The Art of Living with Grief

I wrote
and illustrated this book
for you
and me
with love and compassion
in Memory of
Ben Chappel
my son

Copyright © Claudia Chappel 2018, 2019
Registration number TX 8-697-850

All rights reserved. No part of this publication, including but not limited to artwork and photographs, may be reproduced, stored in any retrieval system, or by any means, without the prior permission in writing by the author.

First published by South Son Publishing, LLC™
Commerce Center-East Building
1777 Reisterstown Road, Suite 355
Baltimore, Maryland 21208

ISBN 978-1-7339047-0-4 (paperback)
ISBN 978-1-7339047-1-1 (hardcover)
Library of Congress Control Number: 2019938792

In this book the author is simply giving a voice to the lessons she learned as she has come to terms with the loss of her son. She is not a trained psychiatrist, doctor, psychologist, grief counselor, or health care professional. She is not giving medical or psychological advice or counseling.

Please visit www.claudiachappel.com

Production assistance by Adam Robinson of Good Book Developers

The Art of Living with Grief

Claudia Chappel

South Son Publishing™
Baltimore

I am grateful to Nancy & Alan Gilbert for their care in photographing and preparing my art for this book; to Cari Stein for her editing, encouragement and sage counsel; and to my husband, Richard Winelander for his help.

Claudia Chappel
Winter 2019

You wake up to another day without your precious child.

You have your entire life to grieve this unthinkable loss.

You don't have to do it all today.

Another day of immense pain and
sadness.
The pain of losing your child will never leave you
and in many ways,
you really don't want it to.

Trust me when I tell you this.
You will get stronger and you will be able to carry it.

It will feel lighter
eventually.

Anger

It's so understandable to feel angry.
I think it's part of the journey toward acceptance
but it is so uncomfortable
and painful.
We don't know where or how to vent it
or who to vent it at.
I remember feeling mad at everyone
for everything
all the time.

When it first happened I announced
that I was never doing anything I loved again.
No more art, no more laughing, no more dancing.
I was going to just let myself fall asleep one day
and not wake up.
My heart and soul were totally broken
and my body would soon follow.

Then I realized what this would do to my daughter
and had to give up that thought.
I have another child who I love
who lost her brother.

In the early months
I remember feeling so nervous and anxious all the time.
I think I was waiting for the pain to subside.

When I realized that this hole in my being,
this unimaginable loss was forever,
I relaxed a bit.
Knowing that the pain
of losing my son would never leave me,
all that pressure I was putting on myself to feel better
lifted.

Friends.
They just don't know what to say.
Some of them, in an attempt to help,
say the most stupid things.
Try to forgive them.
They mean no harm.

It's such a natural instinct
as a parent
to feel responsible when your child dies.
Isn't it our job as parents to
protect our children?
It is a normal thought response,
but it's a deadly one.

Let it go!

The Holidays

The holidays present a new challenge.
We remember these days as busy and full of fun.
Now we watch all the busyness and
excitement all around us.
It's hard to avoid.

The lyrics, "home for the holidays..."
My kid isn't coming home for the holidays anymore.

It's okay to cry. It's really sad.
Again, as you get stronger, joy will slowly start to return.

In time.
Be patient.

Birthdays are hard.
So are anniversaries.
Actually, I find the entire month
of these momentous days
really difficult.

Try to be especially kind
and nurturing to yourself through
these days.

They will pass.

This bears repeating.

It's such a natural instinct
as a parent to feel responsible
when your child dies.

It's our job as parents
to protect our children, right?
It is a normal thought response but in this case,
it's a deadly one.

Please let it go!

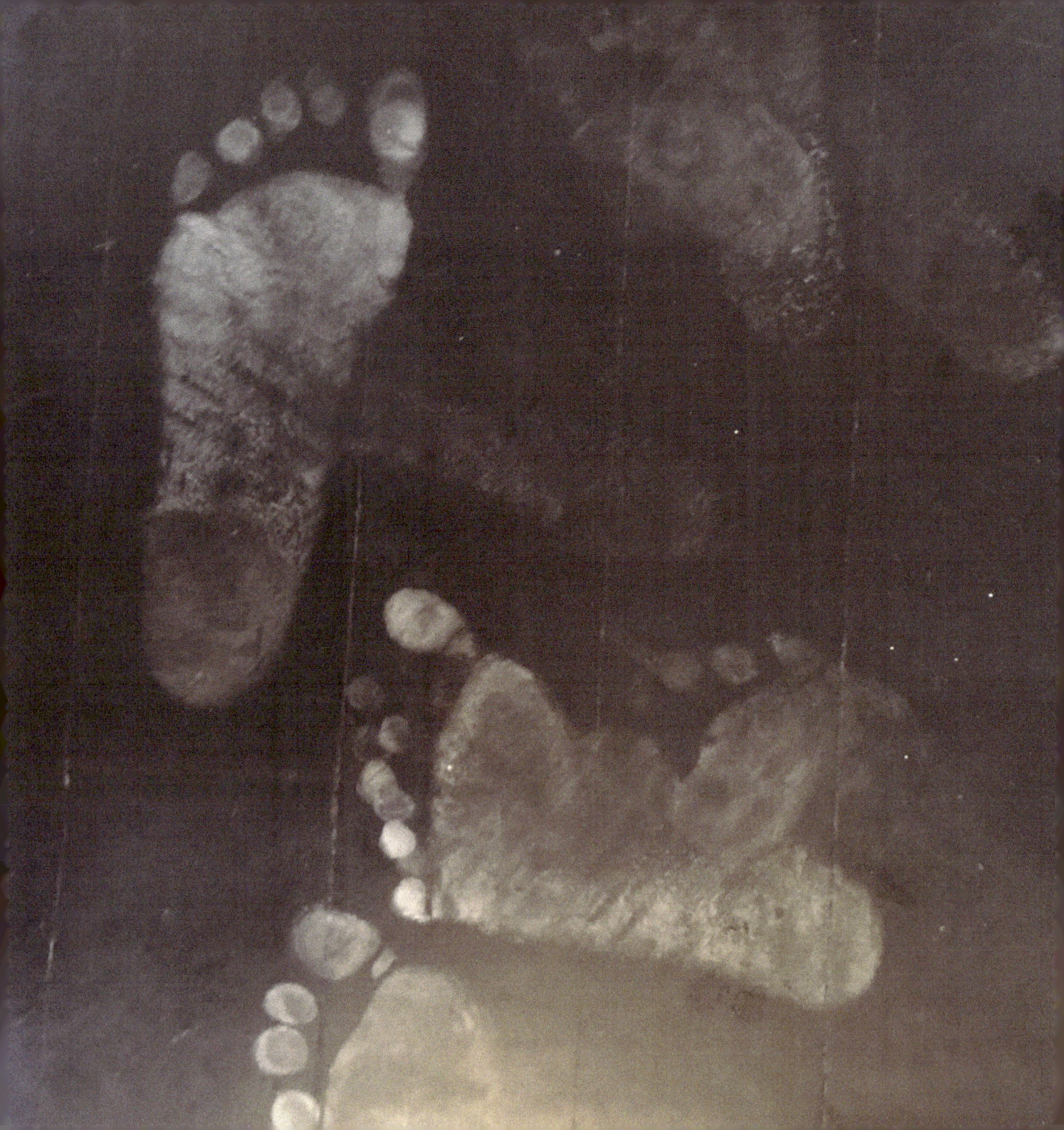

Fear of Loss

It's understandable after losing your child.
I hate when my daughter goes almost anywhere.
I get nervous when my husband is late coming home.
I wake up every morning and check to make sure
my old dog is breathing
or my birds are on their perches
and not on the floor of their cage.

I accept this craziness because I know I am not crazy.
I have experienced and live
with the worst possible nightmare
any parent could ever have.
I accept that my reality is challenging.
I accept that fear of loss is my new normal.
I won't let it paralyze me.
I still have a life to live and people I love
who need me.

Life is short,
we've been hearing this forever.
That phrase takes on a new meaning now.
I remember a morning shortly after my son died
(a word I still can't say out loud).
I was dying inside.
I walked into the living room
where my daughter and husband were just sitting and staring.
I realized that, not so much for me but for her,
I had another choice to make.
I had to set an example for my daughter and my husband.
I made an announcement
that we were going to live out the rest of our lives vibrantly
and had to adjust our voices to sound alive.
We really had no other choice.
I refused to allow my young daughter
to spend the rest of her life not living.

Accept the comfort of your pet.
My dog saved me.
He sensed my pain and never left my side.
I needed a physical being to cling
to who I felt safe with
and who wouldn't feel smothered by my neediness.

I had all this love and pain
with no one to express it to in my desperate state.
I think it's called transference,
but it sure worked for me for a long time.

Animals are the best!
Thank god for them.

It took me weeks to leave my house.
My first outing was Sam's Club with my husband.
I went to the bathroom and on the sink
was a huge pile of pennies.
It was crazy.
I waited for the other woman to leave so I could scoop them up.
My son used to toss loose change on his table in his apartment.
I knew this was him letting me know he was near me.
I have been seeing and collecting pennies from him for years.
I keep them in a special pouch.
Look for the signs.
They may not be pennies, but they are there.
They are near too.
They love and miss us also.
I believe we will be together again one day.

Living life in the light has become more important to me now.
I know that my son is there.
If I want to feel his presence and be with him in spirit
then I have to resonate
where he is.
What keeps me in the light is doing my art,
practicing yoga, spending time with
people I love who love me back,
and surrounding myself with positive energy.
I have let certain people go.
I have no tolerance for drama. I hate crowds and chaos.
This is me.
Find what works for you. Find what keeps you
in the light and
you will find your child there.

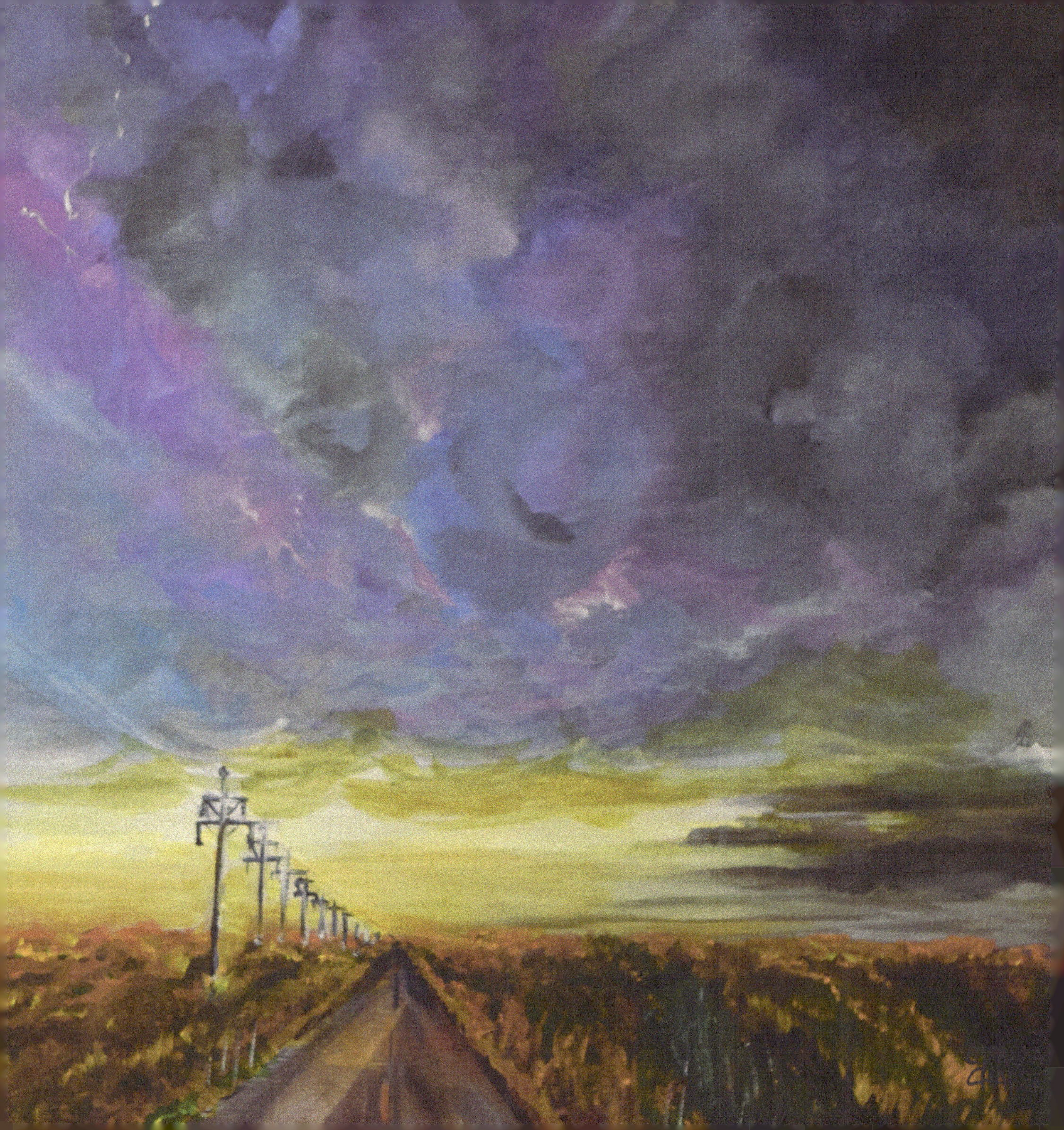

Something will trigger a breakdown.
It could be anything.
A television commercial, a song,
a person on the street that looks like your child.
Anything.
You fall back to square one.
Let yourself grieve.
Let yourself cry.
After,
you can pick yourself up again
and take a step forward.

It's still your time to live and you have a lot to live for.
Yes you do.

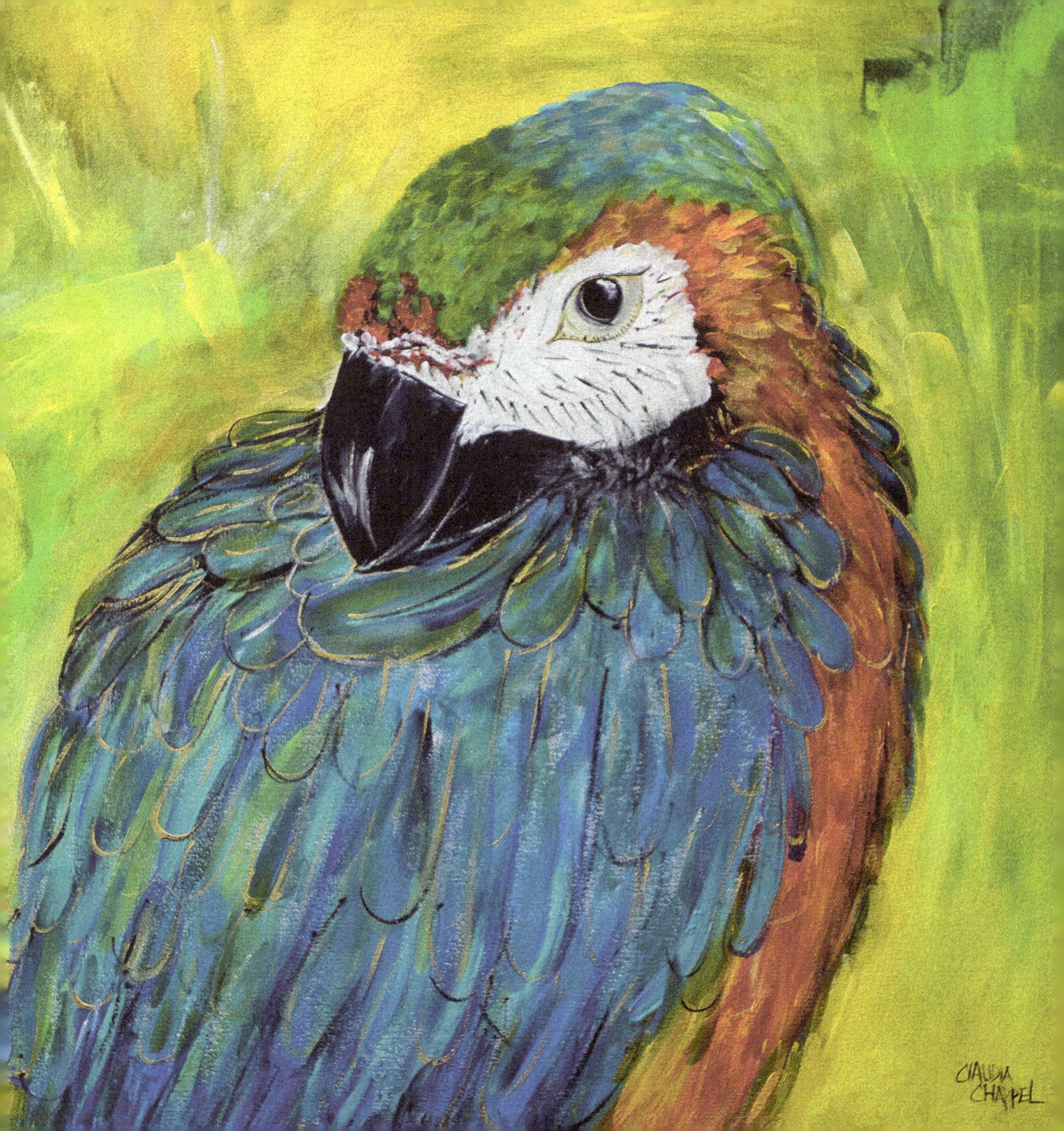
CLAUDIA
CHAPPEL

Don't you hate
when people cock their head to one side and say
in that voice
"how are you???"
I sure do.
How do they think I'm doing?
Again,
they mean no harm.
They just don't know what to say
and how could they?
Try not to let it ruin your workout or your dinner
or your day
or whatever else you're doing to try to live.
This takes strength and time.

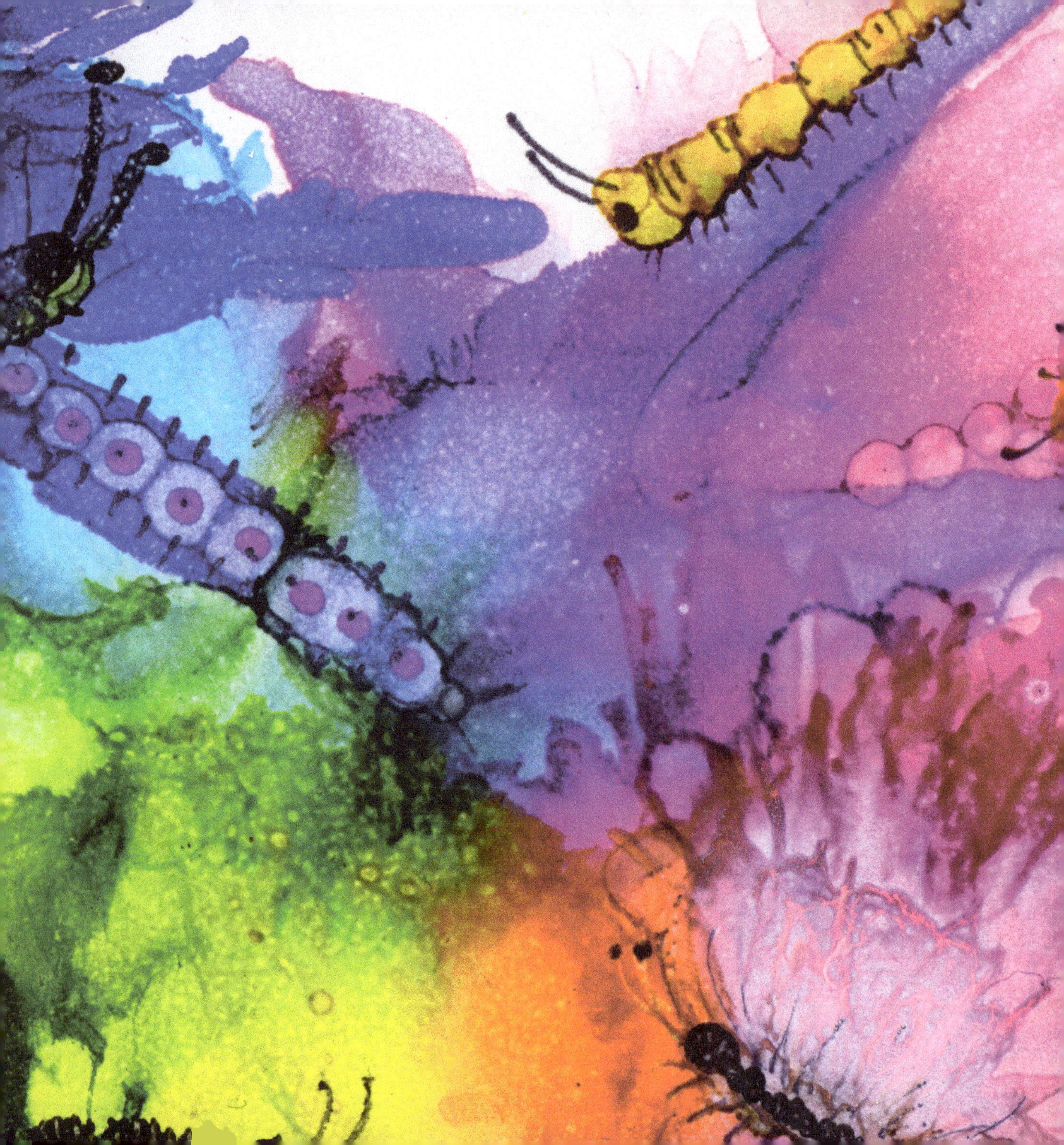

What do you do with their stuff?
It's such a personal decision.
Do whatever you need to do.
I kept tissues that I found in his pockets.
I kept anything that had his handwriting on it.
I still do.
It took me years to finally donate his clothes
and shoes, but I knew he'd approve.
You do whatever you need to do
and
take as long as you need to take.

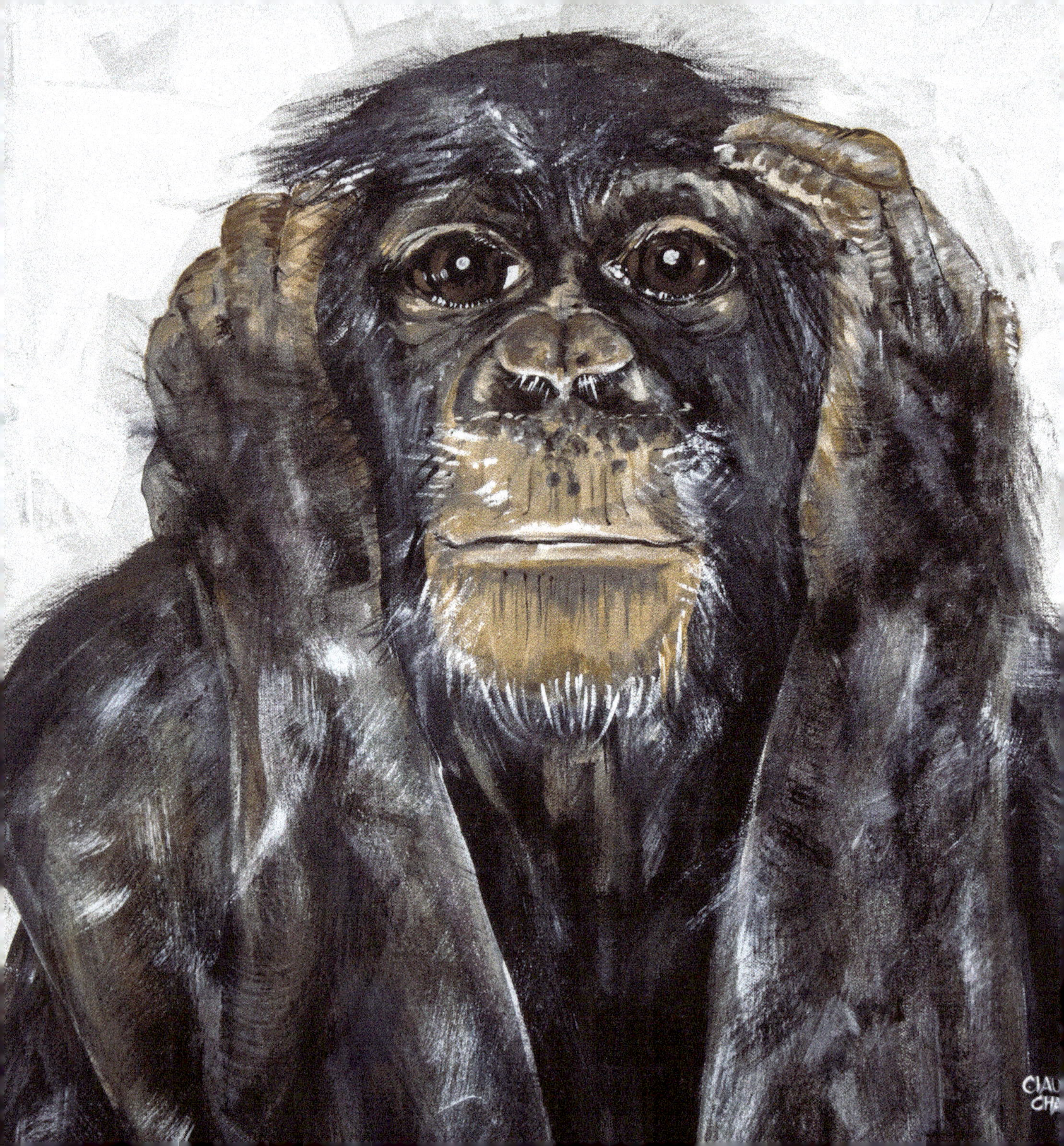

Random people will see you at the grocery store
or wherever and ask about your children.
That's hard. Be prepared.
You can tell the truth or lie.
Sometimes they knew and forgot
or actually didn't know.
People forget, believe it or not.
It's the most horrible event in your life but not theirs.
Handle this however feels okay to you.

There are no rules in this new
reality except survival.

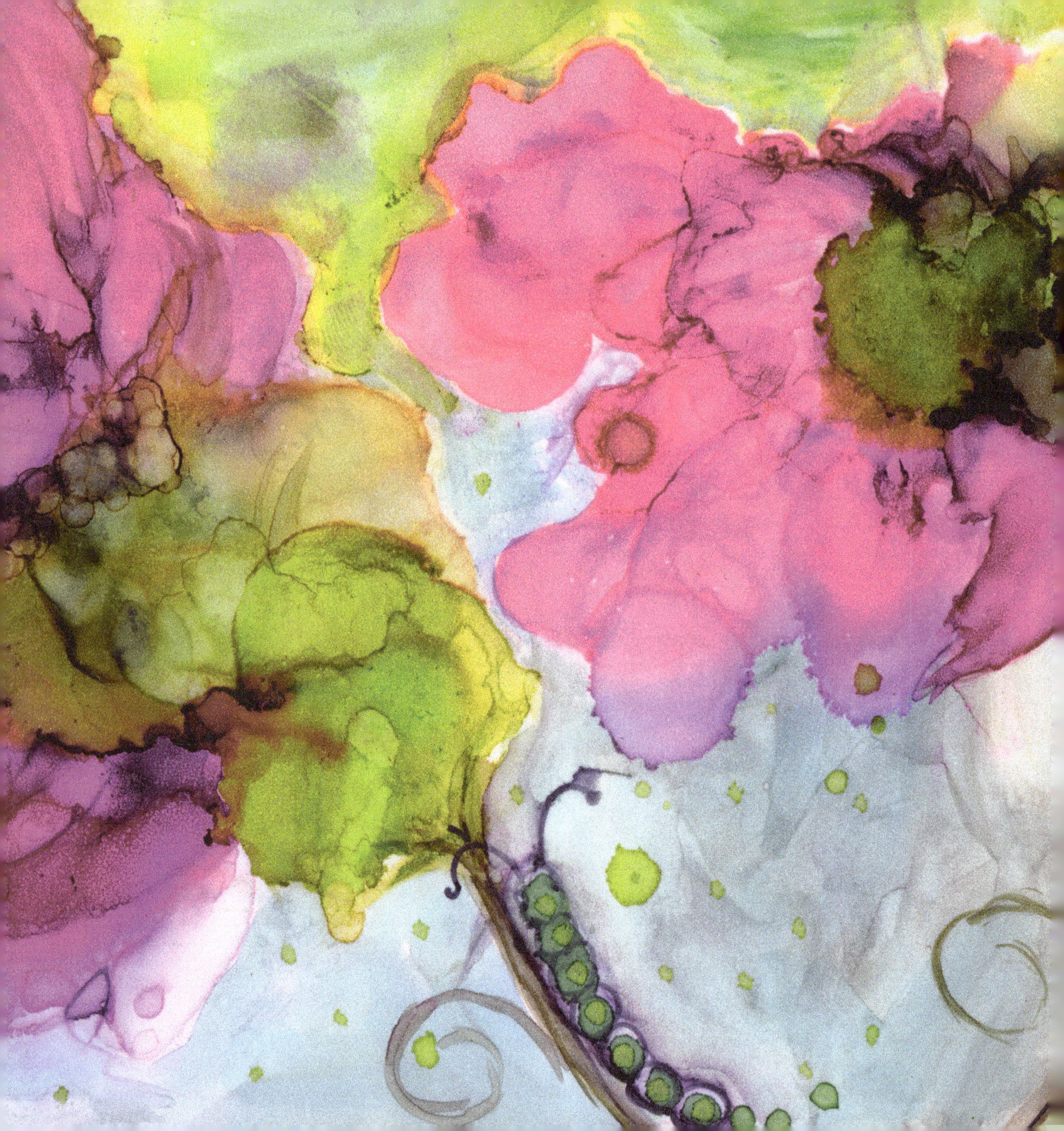

Gratitude

It's not the first word or emotion that comes to mind
these days,
I'm sure.
As you start to accept this horrendous reality,
try to open your minds eye
to what you have not lost.

We again, have another choice to make.
Do we live in deprivation or gratitude?
Gratitude for our other child
or if you are really blessed, children,
grandchildren,
husband or wife
and the love all around us.

I had an incredible dream one night.
I was running towards a vibrant and beautiful sky of blues, greens and purples.
I felt an amazing sense of euphoria.

My husband was far behind me yelling for me to come back. He was yelling "it's not your time yet." So, I turned around and started running in the other direction.

The sky was again vibrant except now the colors were pinks, reds, oranges & purples. Magnificent!

This sense of euphoria was like nothing I had ever experienced in my life. I woke up and realized that my son took me to where he was and wanted me to feel what he was now feeling.

He always did that.

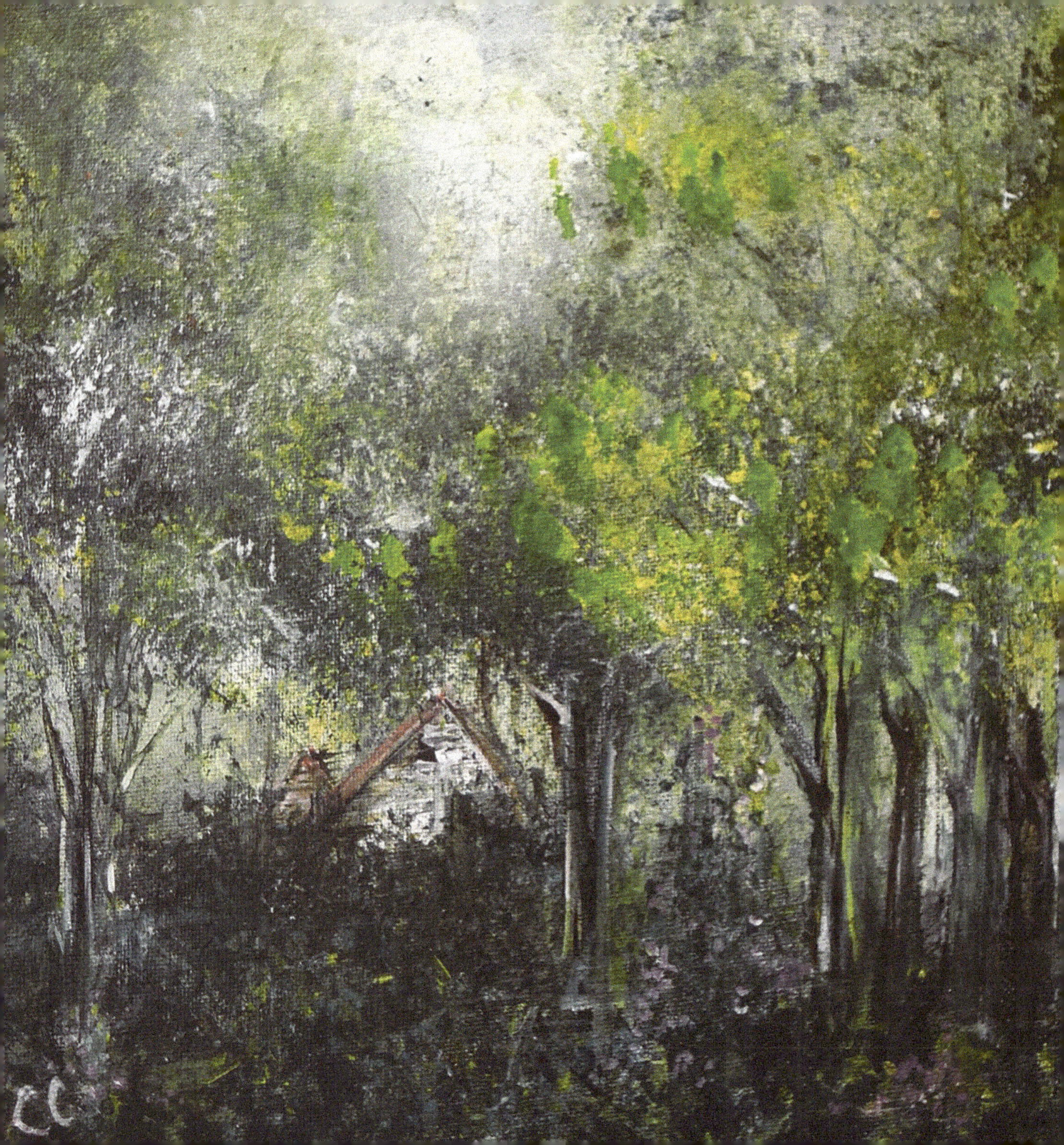
CC

On the morning after I woke up
from that experience I wandered
down the hall of my house.
The sunlight was streaming in.
I actually said to myself
"what a beautiful day"
and then remembered. I was
shocked at the thought.
That's when I realized that my son was
in the light, not in the darkness.

If I could keep myself in the light, I
would feel his presence there.

Benjamin Chappel
1979–2006

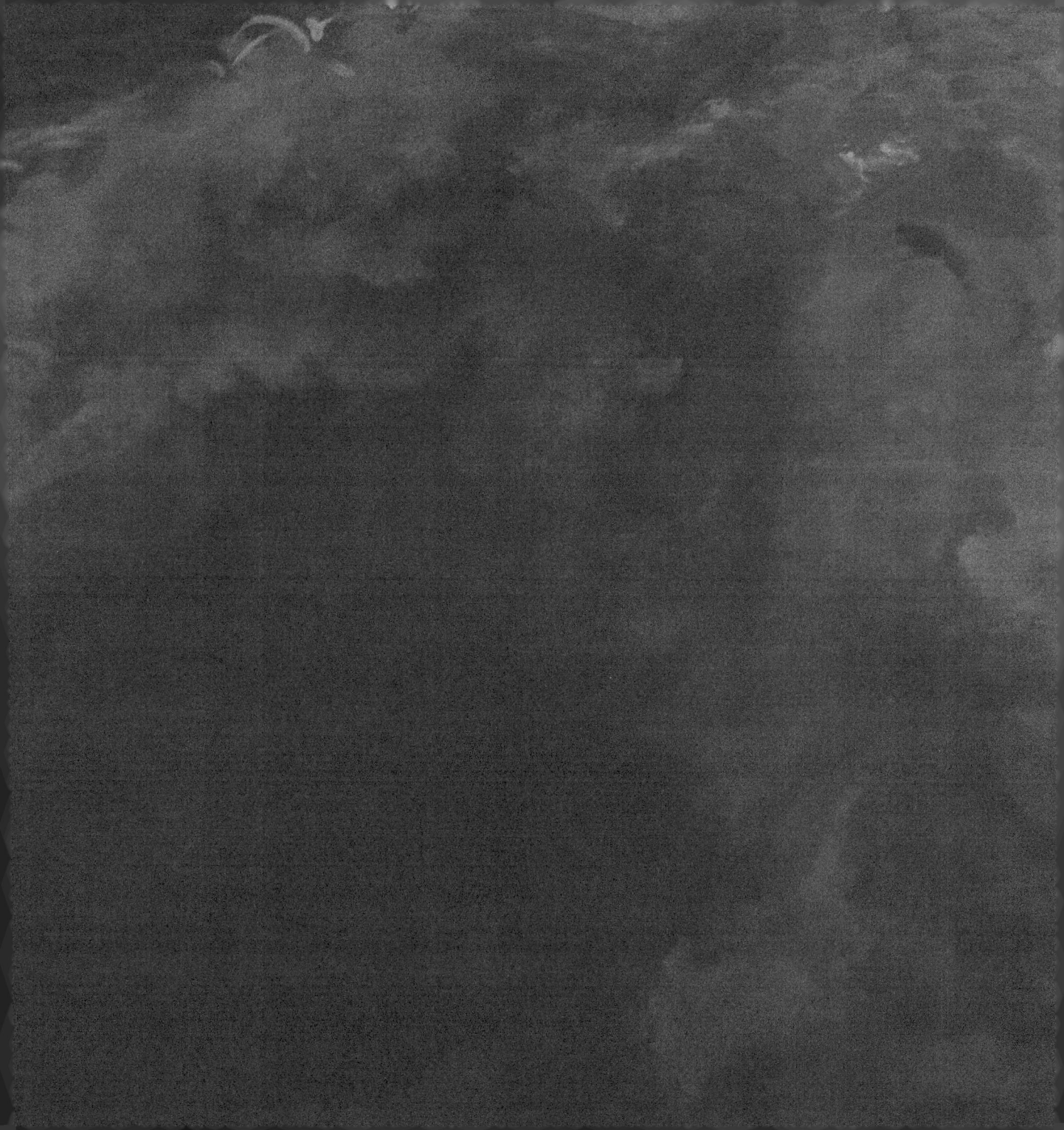

ABOUT THE AUTHOR / ARTIST

A successful professional artist, Claudia, a single mom, supported her children by painting tiles for peoples' houses. It allowed her to be home with her children. At the age of 53 Claudia experienced the unimaginable. She answered a knock at the door and a policeman was standing there. He told her every parent's worst nightmare, her son Ben, the first love of her life was gone.

After Ben's death, she fell into a dark and lonely place. She gave up painting. Over the next 13 years, Claudia slowly learned to live with her pain and grief. She began to paint again. Her work had no special meaning to her at the time.

Parents who have experienced the death of their children began to seek her out for advice, comfort and hope. Over time she realized that she was saying the same words repeatedly. She decided to write them down. It wasn't until she began writing this book that the art, she thought had no meaning, served to be perfect illustrations.

The book was initially written as a gift for a mother whose son had recently died. Other's wanted copies to send to friends who were suffering the same losses. She started making copies.

She discovered that helping other grieving parents gave both her grief and her art a purpose.

Claudia lives in Baltimore, Maryland with her loving husband Richard and close to her daughter Jessica, son-in-law Michael and two grandchildren, Olive and Gus. Her loves also include her two dogs and two birds.

CPSIA information can be obtained
at www.ICGtesting.com
Printed in the USA
LVHW070953220919
631865LV00017B/263/P

WITHDRAWN